42 Rules of Cold Calling Executives

By Mari Anne Vanella

E-mail: info@superstarpress.com
20660 Stevens Creek Blvd., Suite 210
Cupertino, CA 95014

First Printing: May 2008
Second Printing: November 2008
Paperback ISBN: 0-97-994282-9 (978-0-9799428-2-2)
Place of Publication: Silicon Valley, California, USA
Library of Congress Number: 2008921918

eBook ISBN: 0-97-994283-7 (978-0-9799428-3-9)

Trademarks

All terms mentioned in this book that are known to be trademarks or service marks have been appropriately capitalized. Super Star Press™ cannot attest to the accuracy of this information. Use of a term in this book should not be regarded as affecting the validity of any trademark or service mark.

Warning and Disclaimer

This book is designed to provide insight and commentary on marketing principles and practices. You are urged to read available material, learn as much as possible about marketing, and tailor the information to your individual needs. For more information, see the many resources in the section titled "Interesting things to read and do." You can always visit the website at http://42rules.com.

Every effort has been made to make this book as complete and as accurate as possible, but no warranty of fitness is implied. The information provided is on an "as is" basis. The author and the publisher shall have neither liability nor responsibility to any person or entity with respect to an loss or damages arising from the information contained in this book.

If you do not wish to be bound by the above, you may return this book to the publisher for a full refund.

Endorsements

"Mari Anne's 42 Rules are practical, well thought out and show her obvious breadth of experience. She is very good at pointing out how a salesperson with any level of telephone experience can apply strengths that they might have in everyday interactions to becoming a more effective cold caller."
Garth Moulton, Co-Founder, Jigsaw

"The 42 Rules of Cold Calling Executives is one of the most powerful toolsets for both Sales Reps and Sales Development Reps to improve and sharpen their cold calling results immediately. Mari Anne's expertise and talent taps into the areas that affect the overall dynamic of the calls and reveals the formula for success."
Barb Nichols, Independent Consultant and Director of Sales Operations with Vindicia

"This should be required reading for salesreps."
John Sovik, Director of Sales, Kalido Software

Read some of Mari Anne's LinkedIn recommendations:

"Mari Anne Vanella is one of the most prolific demand generation experts that I have had the pleasure to work with. She is "master and commander" of the cold call - if one can call it that - because she invariably turns up hot leads! Her ability to penetrate the CXO domain in Corporate America is simply fantastic."
Jack Nargundkar

"When I started working with Hubspan the company was in dire need of sales leads. Mari Anne expertly provided much needed guidance, and quickly turned around the company's cold calling efforts and greatly bolstered the pipeline. Without her skill, guidance, and strong team the company would not have been able to close more than $3M in new revenue."
Shannon J. Yost, Marketing Consultant

"Mari Anne has an exceptional talent for creating successful Telesales processes and results. I have followed Mari Anne's work over the years, and have seen the positive results her team brings. Mari Anne and her capable team brings strategy and methodology to the table."
Jordan Zweigoron, Sr. Director, Business Development, Genius, Inc.

"Mari Anne is the consummate professional. She really understands the pains of demand generation rather than the lip service and hackneyed processes provided by so many companies in her field. Mari Anne holds herself accountable to results, not activities, and the leads we received paid for her services 20 times over. I have nothing but the highest praise for Mari Anne and her company."
Robert G. Kelly, VP Global Marketing and Alliances, Infogain Corporation

See Mari Anne's LinkedIn profile at:
http://www.linkedin.com/in/vanellagroup

Publisher

- Mitchell Levy
  http://happyabout.info/

Executive Editor

- Laura Lowell
  http://superstarpress.com/

Cover Designer

- Cate Calson
  http://calsongraphics.com/

Copy Editor

- Teclarity
  http://teclarity.com/

Dedication

To Leanne and Ted because they are great people, and I am proud of them.

To my Dad because he gave me such a positive outlook on life.

To Beatrice because she put me here.

Acknowledgements

There are so many people who have contributed to the creation of this book. I appreciate all of the support and contributions from my family, friends, colleagues, and staff. It would require another book to list all the people and events that have helped me over the years. Even though they aren't all listed here, I have enormous gratitude for all of them.

There are some people who made a big difference over the last year.

To Vicki and Steve Cauvel, who have helped me through all of the fiascos last year and kept me on track. To Bobby Holland, my good friend and editor. To Caron Rakich, Karmon and Louis Walker, Barbara Nichols, and Stephanie Giblin for their support.

To all of my clients, for their support and confidence in me and my company.

To Keith Ferrazzi for his experience and for helping me visualize this book.

Contents

Contents

Foreword by Keith Ferrazzi

I spend my time helping people to reach out to others and build relationships. I consider this to be a key element in achieving success, in both business and personal endeavors. I discovered this principle early in life, as I watched the truly successful and sought to understand their paths. The common denominator in their lives was using the power of relationships so that everyone wins.

In my book, Never Eat Alone, I lay out the specific steps—and inner mindset—that I personally use to connect with the thousands of colleagues, friends, and associates, all people whom I have been able to help who have helped me.

Mari Anne's book focuses on the sales professional who must call customers and prospects to build successful relationships, rather than just make sales. She shows you how you can make every call a win for both parties, by helping you to understand how to think in your calling process, how to see both sides of the conversation, and how to organize your sales activity for maximum impact on your prospects.

Sales leaders must meet the challenges of a changing marketplace, with more competition and tighter margins. The ones who get the contracts are not the ones who push the hardest, but the ones who bring the most value to the relationship. *42 Rules of Cold Calling Executives* provides the guidelines for demonstrating that value from the very first contact. Mari Anne also recommends tools that will help you learn more about your customers, so that they become more than just another routine call. They become people who can benefit from what you have to offer, and who may be able to help you down the road.

Her view is the long view of a business partner, which is in short supply in a quarter-driven business environment. However, this view dovetails perfectly with the view I recommend in all exchanges, that relationships power growth. So, if you have this book, you are a person interested in standing out. You have the desire to be successful and will do what it takes. Apply the advice in this book to your sales efforts and you will get there.

I believe you will find her experience and expertise valuable as you navigate your career and this will become an integral part of your professional library.

Keith Ferrazzi
Author of "Never Eat Alone"
http://www.keithferrazzi.com

Introduction

Despite the advancement of sales processes and tools, the abundance of marketing and communication media, and the overall proliferation of the Internet, cold calling is still a big part of building the sales pipeline and will be for many years to come.

For some, the term "cold calling" has many negative connotations. Salespeople sometimes look for ways to avoid cold calling executives, or anyone for that matter. Traditionally, it has been considered a painful part of the sales process, and rightly so, given the rejection, hang-ups, screening, and the push-pull inherent to cold calling.

The good news is that it doesn't have to be that way. You've probably seen people who are very successful in cold calling at executive levels, and with good reason. Cold calling, in and of itself, is not the problem—it is the experience of those on both ends that needs adjustment. Even with all the different methods out there to soften the approach, cold calling remains the most effective manner to reach the people you want.

I built my whole business on the ability to successfully cold call executives. These 42 Rules make an easy-to-use reference guide, and give you something to take away and put to use quickly. My objective is to provide you with effective ways to align your approach to the thinking of the people you are trying to reach, so that you get results.

Some of these Rules will apply to you, and some won't. This book will give you methods to incorporate into your calling efforts. After reading the book, one of my clients said that it is so true that "the little things matter." And they really do; when you talk to people as if they are peers, when you listen, when you acknowledge what's going on within their world, when you demonstrate interest in their accomplishments—it all makes a difference.

You'll see how to build a relationship with a cold call, and you'll realize that it doesn't need to be painful. An enormous amount of information can be shared in a brief call that will help you penetrate the account successfully in a shorter time. Sales cycles can be reduced, and the overall engagement can happen on a much more equitable level by applying these Rules.

I have managed sales organizations for many years and coached countless people on how to neutralize sales resistance in their calls. I wanted to consolidate all my tips into a book that you can keep around as a handy reference, when you want to improve your results. So keep this book on your desk and flip through it when you need to. Ask yourself the question at the end of each Rule and see if you do need to adjust your approach. Don't think that these things are far fetched, because they do work.

This book is for the sales teams in companies like the ones I work with, companies with solutions that are bought at executive levels and require a high-level approach to gain access. I have a lot of exposure to my clients' sales teams, and there are some super smart people out there who will get these points, and some who will struggle because they don't have the tools. This book is for those reps who struggle in some areas, but want results, and want to be proactive about controlling those results.

These are the methods that provide success for my firm and benefits for my clients who subscribe to our programs. I get calls all the time from their sales teams, asking how we connected with executives, when they couldn't. Well, here it is, spelled out in easy-to-read Rules, which you can start using today.

1 Rules Are Meant To Be Broken

2 Tell the Truth

Honesty is not simply the best policy—it's the only policy for maintaining effective relationships.

Calling executives means you are dealing with some of the smartest people in business. Being dishonest will not get you very far. The single biggest mistake you can make is to lie to your prospects. It is the one mistake a client will never forgive.

Starting with a lie, no matter how small, isn't going to lead anywhere good. Even when you encounter an issue that seems small—such as a client asking a question you can't answer—it's better to let them know you don't have the answer offhand than to give them information you'll have to retract later. You can say something like, "Rather than give you bad infor-mation, let me find out and get back to you" or "I am not the right person to have that conversation with; I'll have Joe get that for you." This approach puts you in the role of a valuable consultant, someone to be trusted to give accurate feedback, and provides an opening for a second contact with the client. When you find the answer in response to the query, you can use it as a point of reference when you speak with the client again.

Above all, maintain your integrity. One sales rep interested in selling prospect lists was trying hard to reach me recently. When he finally succeeded, he stated that he had obtained my direct line from my personal assistant, which I knew was a lie.

His dishonest approach ensured that I would never do business with him. A better approach would have been to say he had hoped to speak with me about some of my list requirements. Instead, he chose to manufacture a story about how he was able to reach me, which was totally unnecessary and caused him to lose any access to me in the future.

Another example happened to me recently. "Hi Mari Anne, this is so-and-so," said the caller on my voicemail. "I wanted to ask you a quick question about something." She implied that she was working on something with which I was involved. However, when I called her back it turned out that she was trying to pitch me on something else entirely and she really didn't know me. I felt it was a dishonest way to get me to call her back, and it made me think about whether I want someone like that working with my clients. The tactic worked, but the strategy failed. A better way to handle it is to be confident, say who you are, and briefly state your purpose. You'll get much better results by being confident and to the point, rather than trying to dig yourself out of the ditch of lost credibility.

Using methods that are honest and forthright is what separates professionals from amateurs. Executives are not going to expose their company to somebody who uses an underhanded tactic to gain an objective. Your clients have to know you have their best interests in mind at all times.

On the other hand, you don't have to give a dissertation when trying to contact a prospect. Say what you need to say and be honest about it. If the receptionist asks why you are calling, you can say, "I'm with ABC Company and I'm calling to ask Bill about some planning around his financial systems." Mention specifically the things you want to talk about but don't go into great detail.

As you go through these steps, be aware of where you may be having problems with your process. You will want to always improve your process, fixing any areas where results break down and do not get you where you want to go.

What are your methods for gaining access?

3 Maintain the Right Attitude

Your attitude controls your results.

I read years ago, in a book called *Think and Grow Rich*, about how *thoughts* become *things*. In other words, what you think about becomes reality. This applies to almost every aspect of life. I know by personal experience that it applies to cold calling. Your thoughts about cold calling make a huge difference in your results.

If people are not getting results, one of the first things I troubleshoot is how they are interpreting their calls. For example, it is no coincidence that if people view their calls as a nuisance, then they have very little success. If you start with the attitude that the person on the other end of the line doesn't want to receive your call, your approach will be tentative, and your client will sense your lack of conviction. Without the confidence necessary to effectively promote your products/services, you will spend the rest of the conversation trying to convince the client, against his or her will, to commit to an appointment.

A poor approach will not only disrupt your call, it can completely prevent you from making that initial important contact with a potential client. One sales rep for a large telecom company told me that he regarded leaving voicemail messages as a waste of time. "Why would they want to call me back?" he asked. I have no doubt that the lack of conviction in his approach was communicated in his message in some form. He is absolutely right: what client *would* want to call him back? Put yourself in the executive's place: You get a call from a rep at a database company every three months, and her voicemails sound apathetic, as if this is simply an obligatory follow up. As that executive, would you call her back? Probably not, because you have no cause to think she has anything valuable to offer.

Approach each call from the client's point of view. Take some time and think about what a client needs before making the call; asking questions during the call is also a great way to gather information. You are playing a positive role in every manager's search for the best solutions, and your approach should convey information tailored to that manager's specific issues. Companies expect to be approached with ideas. To be effective, be prepared, confident, and offer relevant information.

The most important task is to identify the problem that your potential client is having, so you can provide the solution. That means learning to listen. Approach the conversation as an interactive transaction, meaning that you have to ask questions in order to find out what the prospect needs. Then listen carefully to the client's responses. Once the prospect identifies the problem, then you are in a perfect position to recommend the remedy.

When you take the appropriate steps, you will find that cold calling can be positive and rewarding to the extent that you bring a client-centered approach to your work. Remember, your internal dialogue will manifest externally. Your attitude must be one of confidence, reflecting your belief that you are providing something of great value to your clients. Get it out of your mind that people don't like sales calls—what they don't like is a *bad* sales call. Think of how you are becoming part of their businesses and providing solutions that will make their jobs easier and more productive. Believe that you have a right to call.

What is your attitude towards your cold calling efforts? Do you need to change it?

4 Always Follow Up

Don't easily quit trying to reach a prospect.

Perhaps one of the biggest complaints I hear is some version of "We left them a message, but they never called us back." It is self-deluding to assume that prospects will call *you* back, although you can be pleasantly surprised on the occasions when they do. It is far more effective to assume prospects will *not* call back. Because you are selling a product or service, the responsibility for making a connection and then following up on it is solely yours.

The task of identifying prospects, assembling appropriate contact information, and identifying an actual level of interest requires far too great an investment of resources to allow success to depend on the whim of busy people. Generally, the prospects will have every intention of returning a call but simply become sidetracked by other responsibilities. Put yourself in a prospect's shoes. Prospects are constantly interrupted, distracted, or confronted with unforeseen emergencies and have to prioritize their time accordingly. Returning sales calls may not be high on their to-do lists. It isn't that they aren't interested; they just need you to pursue them to keep the dialogue going.

If a client doesn't call back, never take offense or assume interest isn't there. You don't want to read anything into it. As far as you know, the client could be busy, out of the office, or sick. A better follow-up model is to reach out every day to see if you can catch clients at their desks and a couple times a week just to leave a message. "Hi, this is so and so with XYZ Company. I left you a voicemail the other day, and I don't know if you got a chance to get to it. I was calling because...." You can end the message with a brief reminder about the discussion you had or what it was that generated the initial interest. When you finally make contact, the client will know who you are. Your voicemail serves the purpose of letting clients know you are trying to connect and it keeps your name fresh to them. They may or may not call back—but don't give up.

Another good practice is to date stamp your calls so you know where you are with the prospect. Don't quickly set a prospect aside until you have made contact, no matter how many attempts you have to make. Sometimes you'll find that prospects are passive in their efforts to connect with you, but there is still an opportunity there. If you know they have interest, but you are having a hard time reaching them, just "zero out" to their assistants and ask if they are around this week; you may find out they aren't. Executives are busy people. Continue reaching out until they call back or you reach them at their desks. Don't leave anyone hanging. Passivity on your end is a key to failure.

One of my clients is a very large network services provider and one of the sales reps asked me how we get people to call her back. She was amazed at how we could get through to people whom she was unable to reach. I told her that we call every day and leave a couple of voice-mails a week. Within a few days of adopting this approach, she connected with someone who had been very difficult to reach and had discussed the opportunity she was pursuing. He actually returned her call—proving that consistent effort gave her the result she wanted. Remember, it is not the prospect's responsibility to make the contact happen, it is yours.

How consistent is your follow up? Do you follow up on all your leads?

Be Diligent

Nothing can take the place of perseverance.

Diligence is defined as "Conscientiousness in paying proper attention to a task; giving the degree of care required in a given situation; persevering determination to perform a task." Diligence is an invaluable asset to help you meet your sales goals. Success in sales does not depend on luck but on building valuable skills. Of all the skills you will learn, diligence is most crucial to success.

Diligence is required for every aspect of a cold calling effort. When you begin any new activity, you must spend a certain amount of time practicing and refining your technique until you are truly proficient at it. A sales rep must fine tune his or her presentation until it becomes second nature. You don't want to adopt a "one size fits all" approach. Being proficient doesn't mean being glib; you have to be able to tailor your technique to a specific client's needs to hold that client's attention.

In our industry, "It's all about the numbers" is a familiar slogan about selling. Nevertheless, salespeople in many call-based prospecting efforts fail to make enough calls. Many consider it tedious work and an unwanted chore. They'll claim it is wasted effort, but in reality there weren't a lot of calls being made and the process used to manage the calls that were made was poor and ineffective. The typical refrain from salespeople is that their results did not mirror their "effort," which is basically a way of convincing themselves that the fault lies in the task, not in their technique. If you find yourself thinking this way, then your frustration might cause the number of calls you make to decline or disappear. However, if you used a process that gets results, you would be inclined to make more calls.

I did some consulting work for a large enterprise software company a few years ago. The manager lamented to me that his salespeople would sometimes turn in a daily call log with as few as six outbound calls on it. "What have they been doing all day?" he wondered. Maybe they were compiling and refining call lists, arranging files, learning new software, reading industry reports, and checking competitor information. These are all commendable activities, but not when the numbers fall. With cold calling, there is no substitute for just doing it. I eventually identified this software company's problem; it lacked a defined process for managing its outbound calls. As a result, no one wanted to make these calls, because doing so wasn't productive. However, putting in an effective, repeatable process for outbound calls made the difference, and the salespeople responded by making more calls.

You want to keep outbound calls at a very consistent level. This consistency has many payoffs. You are building your pipeline, and forming long-term business relationships that you can develop over time and include in your pipeline. For managers, this means establishing processes that are both measurable and repeatable in order to prevent salespeople from filling their schedule with ancillary activities. For the individual salesperson, it means becoming a self-starter and setting aggressive goals without the need for external pressure. No one likes to be micromanaged; when salespeople become proficient at cold calling, they will be proactive in their pursuit and no longer avoid it.

In itself, diligence is no guarantee of success, but lack of diligence will definitely guarantee failure. So look at your current outbound levels and see how you can devote more time—undistracted—to this effort.

Do you block out time for outbound calls on a regular basis?

6 Gather Prospects from Prospects

Every contact can open doors to new contacts.

New prospects can be one of your most fertile resources for locating other prospects within an organization. Even if a particular discussion does not end in identifying an opportunity, it is entirely reasonable to ask the person you interviewed if it would be appropriate to speak to someone else in the organization. When you originally called prospects, they wouldn't have thought to volunteer this, so it is up to you to ask.

One of my clients has a large enterprise data management solution. This business is made up of many different elements, so if a salesperson has difficulty identifying an opportunity in one department, it doesn't mean there aren't active projects in other departments. In this case, it is important for the salesperson to look for further opportunities by asking if there is anything going on in Finance, Operations, Marketing, Merchandising, etc.

For example, we called on the IT organization of a large semiconductor firm to inquire about its plans to improve reporting accuracy within its business intelligence environment. The person we spoke with said that the company's process is to respond to requests from the different business units within the company, and they didn't have anything they were working on that would be a fit for this solution. The IT organization didn't initiate the changes, but the business groups do. So even though one group didn't have anything it was currently working on, we still asked if the person we spoke with if he knew anyone who might be working on similar projects, and we received the name of someone in charge of reporting in the Finance group. As it turned out, the Finance group was looking for this type of solution, and our client was able to engage the account.

Think of different areas of the business where you can develop an opportunity. Then, the next time you are talking with a prospect, ask what that prospect knows about other areas of the business and if he or she can provide you with a contact person.

Don't underestimate the effectiveness of this technique to uncover potential opportunities in your accounts. If you can truthfully tell new contacts that you were referred by their colleagues, your "cold" call immediately becomes warmer. It lends a degree of familiarity. You are automatically pre-qualified as being worthy of their time.

When you reach your new contact, you might begin with, "Hi Diane, this is so-and-so with Acme Technology Company. I had a conversation with Frank Jones over in Finance, and he thought it might make sense for us to have a discussion, based on some of the things you were working on." The warm introduction will at least get you a few minutes to assess the viability of the conversation.

If your service or solution has application in various parts of the business you've called, don't miss the opportunity to network. People honestly don't mind sending you to others if their experience with you was positive, even if your particular solution didn't match their needs.

Are you in the habit of asking for contacts in other parts of the business?

7 Remember, Prospects Are People

Be yourself—and let prospects be themselves.

You may know people who are intimidated about calling senior-level executives. At times, you may even feel the same way. The truth is that there is no reason to be intimidated by any client. Do not allow titles such as "Senior Vice President" or "Chief of" make you tongue-tied. See yourself as the equal of those you call. Are you limiting your contacts to people who are mid-level in an organization because you feel out of your element at a high level? This attitude could set you up for a lot of extra, unnecessary effort to work your way up the management chain.

Executives are the same people in line with you at the grocery store, at the same parent conferences you attend, sitting next to you at the movies. In an environment where their title isn't at the forefront, you don't think of them differently at all. While training salespeople, I tell them to talk to potential clients the same way they would talk to one of their neighbors, as this creates the kind of dynamic that leads to a productive discussion. People are comfortable when they feel they are talking to peers; so be a peer.

Most mid-level managers lack the authority to make a decision about purchasing large solutions or services. Most likely, the Vice President or another upper-level manager is the decision-maker and a far more valuable contact.

If you start your dialogue at a lower-level, it can actually complicate your call, because you will have to depend on the lower-ranking manager to make your case or provide access to the person who will actually buy from you. They might be helpful, or they could give your potential buyer an inaccurate introduction to you and your products or services. You can avoid that scenario by calling the appropriate contact yourself instead of working your way up. If the lower-level person is actually your buyer, then it's better to get sent down the chain.

When you are calling executives, you do want to show a proper measure of respect. However, fawning over them will be perceived as insincere and indicates a lack of confidence. Remember, underneath wealth or fame, the most powerful people you meet are simply trying to make their way through the world, just like you. Don't put them on a level that affects your ability to talk with them normally.

On the other hand, an overly casual attitude can put off your prospects. As a matter of courtesy, you want to show the proper appreciation and respect for the time they are giving you. Don't pretend to have a relationship that does not exist. It is critical to always be honest (Rule 2). You can keep a good balance if you picture them as regular people you would meet at any business event.

A person with whom I once worked mentioned that one of the things she learned from me was that calling executives really wasn't a big deal. Even today, her peers are impressed by her ability to gain access to high-level executives. Her response to them is they are people just like her and she really doesn't feel intimidated to call them. She regularly exceeds her sales goals, and this is one of the ways she does it.

Do you think of yourself on the same level as the executives you call?

8 Don't Give Up

Press through initial sales resistance to real opportunity.

Executives who field several sales calls every day naturally develop resistance to most attempts to get their attention. It's the only way they can stay focused on their priorities, and they have many ways to avoid taking your call. It's almost a knee-jerk reaction on their part; you have to factor that into how you deal with their responses in order to avoid missing an opportunity.

One of the most effective ways that executives end a call before it can really begin is by telling salespeople to "mail me some information." While such a request might be genuine, in almost every case, the intent is to terminate the discussion. Once you agree to send information and hang up the phone, you've lost control of the situation and now you are waiting for them to read what you sent and respond.

What can you do when someone asks you to send information? An effective way to handle such resistance is to say, "Sure, I'll do that, but let me ask you..." and resume your discussion. Be sure that your questions show some knowledge of their business. At that point, you can begin probing for substance. Then, listen for a problem that your particular solution will address.

The prospect may resist because they are expecting a "pitch," but if you engage them in a substantial conversation about their problems, it can provoke a real dialogue. In some cases, the purpose of your initial call will be to gather information and gain an understanding of what is going on in the account and whether there is an opportunity for further discussion. Preparation on your part is imperative, because it allows you to ask pertinent questions.

Instead of starting your call by talking about your product or service, talk about the particular area or technology that you have in common. Ask questions like:

- Are you working on anything in (a particular area)?
- Do you have any issues with (something your products handle)?
- Are you currently able to deliver (something related to your products/services) to your customers?

These questions are intended to spark a response in the client, so it occurs to them that you may be able to help with their current issue or problem. Probing questions open the door for you to explore their issues, identify the specific solution you are providing, and determine the next steps. The bottom line is, *never* give up on the conversation until you know it truly isn't productive. Even in that case, you can still get an idea of when you can re-engage.

Can you make a list of questions that you will use to move a sales conversation past resistance?

9 Don't Take the First "No" for an Answer

Ask the same question in different ways.

Preparation is a key to successful cold calling. Obviously, you must know your own business, but you should also know as much as possible about those you are calling. Rule 8 addressed ways to move past initial resistance by asking knowledgeable questions. Therefore, as part of your preparation, it is important to have prepared different versions of the same question.

Prepare questions based on the areas where you might be able to provide solutions (networking, products, outsourcing, services, etc.). Then put together questions that correspond to a subset of each area. These questions might target a specific element of your solution or a general issue within the industry. The prospect may be looking at a problem from a different perspective and not immediately see the value that your solution could bring. It is up to you to reframe the discussion by asking the right questions so you can get to the real problems your prospect is trying to solve. You can then put your solution in that context.

Suppose you are talking about network infra-structure, and you ask your prospect if his company plans on updating its Wide Area Network (WAN). If the response is no, rather than let the conversation end there, ask the same question a different way. Narrow it to something specific about a single area of networking activity, such as "What are you using for broadband access right now?" Narrowing the scope of your question gives a prospect a different perspective. It helps you direct the conversation so you can gather the information you need and gives you the opportunity for further discussion.

The point is simple—do not read the first "no" as a "no opportunity." But that doesn't mean it is easy. By asking more questions and narrowing the scope of your questions, you might discover that "no" could have many meanings. It could simply mean "not now" or "not that." Rather than being an absolute rejection, "no" can actually open doors for an altogether new approach.

Be aware of how your prospects categorize their needs. For example, a company is considering a billing system upgrade. It might be looking at a data standardization project rather than a stand-alone data project. Knowing something about its business can help you uncover potential areas where you can contribute to the company's success. And it also helps you to reposition your questions based on the company's perspective. Through preparation, you can find your way past the "no" to determine what a company really needs.

In working with Borland Software, one of the things it would usually ask potential customers about is Application Lifecycle Management (ALM). Some potential customers wouldn't think that it had an actual lifecycle management initiative, but the customer may have plans to replace its management solution or its modeling environment. When we asked about ALM, if the response was flat, we would then ask about more specific stages of the application lifecycle. Many times, this inquiry uncovered opportunities to standardize platforms and processes. Borland would be able to develop that sales opportunity because we had been able to uncover a need that wasn't readily apparent.

So, have different views of your solution in your mind when you qualify your prospects. When you broaden your perspective and see issues on their terms, your opportunities are greatly increased.

Can you think of different ways to uncover an opportunity with your prospects?

10 Ask Good Questions

**The right
questions can
clarify a
prospect's
needs and your
solution.**

The person on the phone may initially fail to grasp the connection between what his or her company needs and what you are offering. It is important to know the *right* questions to ask about the particular industry you are involved in.

One of my staff called the CIO of a large manufacturing company regarding a solution for the company's application infrastructure problems. The CIO thought that the company was already solving these problems with its own internal processes and tools. During the conversation, however, it became obvious that the product we were talking about was not the product the CIO thought we were referring to. As we continued discussing the situation, we asked about specific business problems he was having with the company's current environment and industry. By mentioning specific scenarios, we created a way for the CIO to quickly relate to the conversation. He saw, based on our questions, that he did have some open issues he was trying to solve. The fact that we knew about them caused him to want to know how we could contribute. We turned initial resistance into a successful engagement.

Your success in turning a situation like this to your advantage lies in your ability to ask specific questions about specific areas of performance. Ask about the areas that your target executives will recognize as problematic. Learn what their industry lacks as a result of not having your solution. You can create this kind of positive outcome only if you have a good working knowledge of the prospect's business infrastructure and corresponding problems. To speak meaningfully to executives, you need to speak their language and understand their perspective.

Executives think of the business in terms of performance and goals. They are not thinking of features and functions of a solution—they are focused on results and return on investment. Your questions should bring to light the business problems they are facing. To avoid losing focus, design your questions with an understanding of their area of business and with anticipation of the prospect's desired results.

Spending time defining your questions beforehand gives you quick access to topics that you can explore with your prospects. It prevents the conversation from ending prematurely, because you will know how to proceed and keep it moving. When you demonstrate knowledge of the prospect's business, it builds the prospect's trust in you.

A former employee told me that one of the most valuable things she learned is that you don't have to know everything about your solution; you just need to know how to ask the right questions. This way, the prospects will tell you if there is an opportunity available, as opposed to the traditional method of trying to get them to listen to a presentation.

To optimize your results, break down your client base into specific categories based on the nature of their business or industry. You can even do it by their roles, as different parts of a business view problems differently. Keep that in mind when building your question sets; then identify problems common to their environment. Now you can discuss specific point solutions based on their industry-related needs.

While taking this approach, let the prospect do most of the talking; you will see that it gives you enormous advantage. By asking the right questions, you will know exactly what they need.

Do you ask meaningful questions that uncover your prospects' requirements?

11 Be Real

It's much easier to just be yourself.

There are many different ways to begin a conversation. Some people think adopting a false sense of familiarity will ingratiate them to their prospects. Be careful about doing that, especially when no basis for a relationship has been established, as it might come off as pretentious and irritating. It typically has the opposite effect from what was intended. It is probably not how you approach someone you are meeting in person, which is important to note, because there should be no difference from how you are on the phone.

Before a valid relationship has been built with prospects be careful about using bridges like, "How are you today?" or "Do you have a few minutes to talk about...?" It is good to use their names, but don't overdo it; at the beginning and at the end of the conversation is enough. I have heard sales training methods that encourage salespeople to say, "I have a thirty-second message for you; if you like it will you give me another three minutes?" This is not how professionals talk to each other. Such an opening immediately identifies you as a sales call, and the initial response is usually to push back.

Separating yourself from the typical call doesn't require that much effort and makes a huge difference in results. You can build a more normal rapport by being direct, honest, and concise. If the conversation lends itself to it, ask how they are. But be careful. Sometimes injecting bridges like that into your introduction serves as the "Here is your opportunity to end the call with me" cue.

Try a more low-key approach such as "Hi, Steve...this is Mike Smith over at XYZ Solutions. We specialize in security testing for companies like (big client names). I wanted to ask you about the planning regarding your security testing and see if we can talk about possible solutions we offer."

In one ten-second exchange you have:

- shown that you know who the client is and the nature of the client's business,
- cited credible reference clients,
- introduced yourself without being overly familiar, and
- identified your solution/service and its potential value to their business.

The likelihood is that if clients have an active project, they will tell you. They may ask if you work in a specific area they are dealing with, which lends itself to a peer-to-peer conversation. You now have a rapport, and you can speak with assurance and without intimidation.

If the prospect is too busy to talk, the prospect will tell you. Simply ask when to call back. You may run into timing issues, and you will have to call back repeatedly with some prospects, but they'll let you know if you are interrupting something. It is not necessary to start your conversation by asking their permission to talk.

Leading the conversation with your "lighthouse" client names will have a lot more punch than challenging them to like or dislike your 30-second "pitch."

How do you initiate your calls?

12 Keep Detailed Records

Knowing where you have been will move you forward.

Achieving quality in a selling experience depends on keeping an accurate record of every conversation with each client. Knowing what you have done so far and what was said allows you to be as effective as possible. Write everything down. If you rely solely on memory, you will find yourself forgetting important details about past conversations or miss opportunities to re-engage down the road. Time is the enemy of accurate recall.

Keeping good records helps if you are not personally handling the follow-up call. The next caller will need to have historical detail about the client, its business, and what was discussed in previous calls. If one of your colleagues needs to reach out to an account, your notes should clearly show exactly what the prospect said, the results of your call, and the next necessary steps in the process. It is important to capture as much of this information as you can during and after your conversations.

Notes written during the course of business tend to be brief and full of shorthand. However, they should not be so terse or full of personal shorthand that deciphering the meaning at a later time becomes a problem. The more complex the sales transaction, the more critical your notes become. Some field notes are so incomplete that no one can decipher them later, including the author. Notes should be so thorough that follow-up callers don't have to come to you later, asking for interpretation. Instead, notes should be a blueprint of how to proceed further.

By keeping detailed notes, first-line salespeople can become communication channels between the companies they represent and the companies they target for marketing.

Notes in your call record about each project should include these details:

- The prospect's area of business
- The name and title of your contact
- The contact's admin and any attempt to screen you
- The name(s) of the person/people driving the project
- Project goals and any important details about the project
- Additional vendors operating in the same arena and if they've made contact
- Any detail about the prospect's plans and how it plans to move forward

Accurate record keeping helps you avoid revisiting previously discussed details, making you more effective with prospecting, and expediting progress in the account. Ultimately, you will advance in the account much more effectively if you keep track of everything that was said.

Do you understand the value of keeping clear and accurate records?

13 Can You Automate Yourself?

Use productivity tools to gain an advantage.

Your cold calling will yield opportunities at all stages. Ignoring opportunities that may arise in the future is shortsighted. Many times leads go out to the field, and if there isn't clearly a deal in the works, the rep just dumps it. Then when the same rep reaches out to the prospect a year later, the rep finds the prospect working with another vendor and that the chance for a deal has been missed. A better way to manage that problem is to understand when prospects plan to make changes and to make sure you are in dialogue with them at that time. If you automate yourself, with very little effort you can keep track of deals at all stages of the process.

Making the switch to automation is a difficult move for many people. Do you know many people who still keep hard-copy notes of everything? You'll find that when you automate yourself, the ability to increase your coverage is huge, and you'll find that you can make better progress in your accounts by having technology do the work for you.

The Sales 2.0 climate is providing efficient productivity tools to automate redundant or time-consuming tasks. However, too many sales reps continue to use Sales 1.0 methods, using schedule and account-tracking processes consisting of some combination of sticky notes and memo pads. Is that really the best way to achieve a long-term payoff with your cold calling? Many salespeople who sell into technology markets don't use technology to the fullest extent themselves.

Common productivity tools, such as Outlook and Salesforce, can relieve you of manual effort to complete routine tasks. Some people still keep notes on their accounts and hard copies of documents; they are constantly dealing with pieces of paper and the inability to quickly retrieve information. With these technology tools, they can manage information and data far more effectively and efficiently.

Automation will also help with advanced scheduling. I know of a sales rep for a large broadband access provider who called into an account and learned that it wasn't going to consider a particular upgrade for a couple of months. A year later, he discovered that the deal was lost to someone else, because his competitor was actively working the account. Had this sales rep set an alert and called back in sixty days, he could have had an opportunity to participate in the deal. With proper automation, you can now stay on top of deals you may have missed previously. You can now retrieve the information you need when you need it, in the correct form. How many times in your cold calling efforts have you been told that your prospects aren't planning changes for six or nine months? How will you be able to keep abreast of those warm leads within that timeframe?

Smart phones and PDAs have become important productivity tools. When you automate the maintenance of date and contact information, it can free you to concentrate on the tasks that more directly impact your production—like making calls.

Early adopters automated their work more than two decades ago. Sales 2.0 is here, so if you are in the Sales 1.0 mode, it's time to change.

Are you automated with your opportunity management? What can you do to optimize your effectiveness?

14 Develop Relationships

Before you sell, build.

The relationship-building aspect of sales is crucial. Only through that process can you develop a champion within the account, a person on the inside of the target company who is considering your solution and socializing it to others in the company.

Establishing this type of relationship can exert a huge and positive effect on the progress of the account. Failing to establish it, on the other hand, can prevent you from reaching your buyer. I was working with a remote access software company and it had contacted a very large grocery store chain based in the Midwest. During a lengthy conversation with one of the chain's key people, our client learned that the chain was interested in developing a relationship to discuss problems with remote access. The chain was also interested in providing an introduction to decision-makers in charge of projects in that area. This was an opportunity for our client, the software company, to develop a champion in the account; this key person could influence the chain to trust that our client would be able to solve their challenges.

In the follow-up call, the rep began the conversation by saying, "I am following up on your interest in purchasing one of our products." The contact responded that wasn't the case, at which point the rep came back complaining that it wasn't a "credible" lead. What was his mistake here? In the follow-up call, he completely glossed over the earlier conversation notes and recommendations to engage. By not referencing any of the discussion from the initial call, he had completely blown this opportunity to connect through a warm introduction with a potential buyer. In the initial call, the contact did not express interest in purchasing anything; this was clear in the notes. He wanted to lead us to the people in their organization who *would* be interested in purchasing something. He was willing to help make that connection based on his role in the company. He wanted to talk about the challenges they were dealing with in his group.

A better way to approach this prospect would have been to follow up on the initial discussion with the intention of learning what he was working on and then exploring if there was a fit. The next step could have been to introduce the sales rep to the right people in the group. The initial contact person could have answered questions about the chain's requirements, how they had been solving or not solving issues, how to engage with the buyer effectively, if there is a budget, and other similar issues. Much progress could have been made if the first follow-up served to build the relationship.

Start by building the relationship; begin working from the prospects' perspectives. Taking time to really understand their specific issues will set you apart from the calls they receive all day long, pushing meetings and products. Even if there isn't currently an opportunity, you'll have a better chance of being brought in during buy cycles because you took the time to explain how you could help them from their perspective.

Are you building relationships that will pay off?

Rule 14: Develop Relationships

15 Track Leads Carefully

Success is in the details.

There is sometimes a breakdown between sales and marketing regarding leads that marketing generates. You don't want to let those leads "fall through the cracks." When a sales rep first identifies an opportunity, he or she puts forth some effort. But if the prospect doesn't call back right away or as other things come up, the opportunity may cycle off the radar for the rep and be lost to a competitor.

A sales rep for one of my clients, a security software company, was concerned about how difficult it was to get a prospect in the company to call him back. "What's your process for tracking your calling?" I asked him. "I keep the leads in a folder," he replied (this was an actual manila folder, by the way). "Every time I make a call, I mark a little dot at the top of the page. I've got three dots on this page, which means that I called the prospect three times." How could he possibly know what he has done with a dot?

The rep did not know what day or at what time of day he had made any of the calls, whether he had used email or voicemail, or what message he had left. He had nothing on which to base a sales strategy or even enough to maintain substantial coherence in a calling plan.

Most prospects require a lot of repeat calling, especially if they are in a high-visibility role. A large number of calls are usually made into an account before a sales rep can identify an opportunity and follow it to its conclusion. You might make over forty calls in order to connect to ten people, which would identify a subset of active opportunities. If you're working on a number of projects and building on that weekly, the number of calls you make each week will quickly lead to confusion and chaos unless you keep everything sorted through a system of careful tracking at a contact and account level.

One advantage of maintaining a log and detailing every phone call is to permit you to manage the spacing of the calls. In most cases, you will want to attempt to make the contact on a daily basis. This doesn't mean leaving a message daily, but if you know this call has potential, don't leave it up to the prospect to call you back. With a little planning, you can vary the timing. Some prospects are more accessible in the mornings than in the afternoons, for example. If you alter the times you call each day, you increase the odds of catching them at the time they are most likely to answer the phone.

In addition to the date and time of the calls you make, there are other elements you should track. For example, always note the admin's name; this way, during subsequent attempts, you will create a working relationship with the admin. The admin can actually help you reach your prospect at the right time. Building this relationship (yes, it is important) could encourage the admin to assist you in making contact with the boss. You can also note the type of phone system menu you encounter, as that information may enable you to dial by name and circumvent the admin altogether.

Make your calling process as rational as possible. After each attempt, take a moment to consider what you learned from the attempt (including names and/or company info). Note any suggestions that might be helpful the next time you call (like out-of-office info, extensions, alternate contacts) and write down the date and time you plan to make the next call. Maintaining such details in call-attempt records is obviously valuable, especially if you need to contact the person again at some point, perhaps months in the future.

What kind of records do you have of accounts you are working?

16 See Every Project from the Prospect's Perspective

Start selling to prospects only after they tell you what they want.

Salespeople attempt to sell me products that, ostensibly, will help me run my telesales company more effectively. It is extremely aggravating to realize that they are trying to make a sale without bothering to find out exactly what type of business I own or what I require in order to run it. If they approached me in an interactive manner to understand if there is even a fit, then I would tell them what I need, which would lead to discovery on both sides.

You must listen to the prospect. Don't assume that your prospect needs what you have. See it from the prospect's perspective. What is the prospect's business? Do you have other clients to reference in that industry? Can you find out more about what the prospect is doing that can uncover needs it does have?

Let the prospect talk about his or her business. Just listen, and ask questions designed to elicit more details. If you listen long enough, you may find out what is needed. A common failure for salespeople is to attempt to sell a solution when there is not a problem. They are so focused on trying to get through their script that they aren't able to hear the prospect's actual need or interest. Salespeople who fail to address the prospect's needs have to try to dig themselves out of a hole, which isn't always possible.

I once piloted a contact database solution to see if it saved time and effort in our calling effort. I received a call from the rep, who projected some wild numbers about how much it costs for me to get a contact, and how much money his application would save. I said that wasn't what I was looking at. I was looking at time and effectiveness. Not to mention, the numbers he provided were completely inaccurate. My view was that if this application didn't save time, then it wasn't a fit. Then the rep again projected numbers that were made up and not applicable to my business, which I again said didn't apply. After a few calls from this person, I told the rep that he would get much further selling me his stuff if he listened to what I said I wanted. His response was that I couldn't see the value (it was my fault!) because I wasn't letting him demo the product.

So, before you talk about something that doesn't apply, find out how your prospects see your solutions or services. Gain an understanding of what they want. Every company has different requirements, some slight and some significant. Determine how your prospects view their requirements in order to talk to them about the solutions.

In a face-to-face meeting, you have more room to back up and review something if there is a disconnect in the discussion. The prospect may also be in a frame of mind to spend more time exploring a topic. On the phone, especially a cold call, you don't have that luxury; the end of the discussion is a hang up away. Make your words count.

The key to this principle is to use the conversation to identify what the prospect actually needs and adapt your dialogue accordingly.

Can you find a way to see your prospect's vantage point?

17 Use a Script, but Don't Be Scripted

Create content that is compelling, comprehensive, and concise.

Most telesales organizations have scripts, which are sometimes called "templates" or "call guides." They usually begin with some variation of the hackneyed, "Hi, Ms. Vanella! How are you today? Do you have a moment?" You can probably guess how effective this approach is.

These scripts sound canned (yes, but it's a script, right?) and possess a "telemarketing" ring. They never sound the way a real person actually talks, especially when that person has something interesting to share. That kind of canned approach might be effective when you are trying to sell magazine subscriptions or long-distance phone service, but it will never work when you are trying to sell a data-intensive computer grid or a million-dollar cluster system.

I don't write scripts that sound canned, but I do use scripts. I have specific plans for what I intend to talk about in a very natural fashion, using a completely normal tone of voice. The script you use should be in your voice, which will enable you to speak clearly about complicated topics, help you to be thorough in your discussion, and protect you from saying things you never intended to say.

The script establishes flow. You want it to frame how you want the dialogue to proceed and which points need to be covered. The purpose of a well-prepared script is to aid you in remembering the key points you need to cover in your dialogue.

A script also keeps you on track. During the course of a call, your discussion with a prospect may get off topic, and the script can provide a reference point. It saves you from having to try to remember where you are in your presentation and avoid missing points during the call.

I prepare a script for every call I make. I also have a collection of scripts that are modified according to industry and tailored to the role of the prospect in the company. I use a different script when speaking with a CIO than I use when speaking to a Vice President of Logistics. A script for a Vice President of Manufacturing will be different from one prepared for a Vice President of Human Resources.

How should you write your script?

- Write down exactly what you say that gets the best results.
- Have lists of questions or data points you are seeking on your call.
- List some information about your company that your prospects may ask.
- Organize the information by prospect title if necessary.

A good script also becomes a quality control measure. Sometimes, the effectiveness of your calls will decline, and the responses will differ from those you received previously. If your production has declined, you may have changed what you were saying without realizing it. At some point you may have left out something or started saying something new because it sounded good to you. How do you find your way back? Having your original script handy can help you quickly determine if you need to readjust your dialogue. This way, you can create a rational method from your discussions with prospects, which leads to a process of continual improvement.

Do you write down scripts that work and use them for future reference?

18 Be Natural

Transparency and sincerity are keys to successful phone transactions.

Too many salespeople act differently on the phone than they do in face-to-face situations. In some cases, people with dynamic personalities become tense on the phone, casting aside the qualities that might have gotten them the job in the first place. They sometimes regard the telephone as a barrier to communication rather than an effective communication device. To avoid saying things on the phone that you wouldn't say in person, simply speak to the person on the other end of the line as though he or she were standing in front of you.

The notion of being natural in business phone conversations is an area in which expectations have shifted dramatically. A couple of decades ago, people doing enterprise solution and technology sales were expected to behave in a very formal and "buttoned-down" fashion. In those days, business people were expected to maintain a high level of professionalism, one that regarded a call from the person's kids at work to be a breach of expected business etiquette.

Today, industry is genuinely more understanding about human factors in business. This makes it essential that you learn to be yourself while talking to people about business. You will make your point more effectively if you develop your business relationship with the prospect as a fellow person (Rule 11).

Keith Ferrazzi, author of the bestseller, *Never Eat Alone*, points out: "The only way to get people to do anything is to recognize their importance and thereby make them feel important. Every person's deepest lifelong desire is to be significant and to be recognized." This is excellent advice, because you are there to provide a service to the prospect as a future customer.

The effectiveness of your dialogue depends, in part, on your ability to sound natural, not tense. Don't merely say, "How are you today?" Greet the person in a warm and genuine fashion.

When I greet people on the phone, I always mentally envision myself walking up to them and shaking their hands. This is an effective method that assures a seamless transition between the dynamic of in-person and phone introductions. Use actual gestures. You might be surprised, but people can "hear" the gestures over the phone.

Your ability to be natural can determine whether if someone will talk to you or not. The more formal you sound, the more the prospects will feel disconnected from you.

What can you do? Stay in tune to what is going on during the call. Be aware of little things that can put your prospect at ease, and be as warm over the phone as you are in person. I have told people many times to talk to people on the phone as they talk to their next door neighbor. If you can develop that mindset, it changes the whole dynamic of the call.

I receive many calls from salespeople, and the determining factor of whether they gain my attention is whether or not they convey a comfortable, relaxed attitude. Learning to be natural will be a huge part of your success as well.

Are you in the habit of being natural in voice and manner when speaking on the phone?

19 It's Not Always about the Sale

Build the foundation first, and the deal will follow.

All prospects you talk to understand that you are not calling to make friends with them. They know and expect that you are looking for an opportunity to work with them.

Businesses don't sit around waiting for ways to spend money. However, they are always searching for ways to solve their problems. Therefore, the point of your initial call should not be about selling something (getting them to spend), but rather about gaining insights into the prospect's account (understanding their problems). You and the prospect are both determining if there is any reason for further discussion.

You would be amazed at the amount of detail that a first call can gather. The best approach to acquiring account details is a *softer* approach. Your goal is to get prospects on the phone and then to have discussions centering upon their needs. Never try to make a sale where there is no opportunity established.

One of my clients had a network-related solution, which we presented to a nationwide company that sold take-out prepared dinners. In the ensuing conversation, we discovered that this company was using a competitor's products and services. We didn't try to sell anything to them but simply asked about what was going on in their environment. We were looking to find out if they were happy with their current vendor and, if not, what made them dissatisfied.

The prospect spent twenty minutes complaining about the failures and shortcomings of its current provider. The prospect disclosed what was really needed and why the company wasn't committed to working with its existing provider. Although there wasn't an immediate opportunity on this account, we still took careful notes, knowing that when the time came, this company would definitely be open to a solution by my client. This was potentially a $3M dollar deal. However, this company was currently under a contract that wouldn't expire for two years. If we had pressed for a sales presentation, we would have been turned down.

We were effective because we didn't talk; rather, we just let the prospect do the talking. The secret is not to focus solely on a sale. On an initial call, you can learn six things about any prospect:

- What is going on in this company?
- Is there a sales cycle?
- How can we sell against our competitors?
- What are they specifically looking for?
- Who are their chief internal contacts?
- What are they currently paying?

This sounds like a lot of information, but if you aren't trying to sell them, they aren't going to be trying to avoid you, and the dialogue is much more open. Let me assure you, you can usually get most of this in a twenty-minute cold call if your focus is not solely on making a sale.

What do you need to change in your approach in order to focus on the prospect's need and not on the product you're selling?

20 Put Yourself in Their Shoes

It's easier to lead prospects where you want them to go when you understand where they are.

Try to understand where your prospect is coming from. Remember that everyone you are trying to contact is receiving many other calls and voice-mails from people just like you. You have a small window to get a prospect's attention and continue the discussion.

While the prospect may eventually be convinced that the product or service you are offering is important, initially, your call is not a pressing matter to a prospect. It will take time to build credibility, and the way to do it is to discuss something your prospect can understand and connect with right away.

Go into an initial conversation with several things at your fingertips:

- Your prospect's role within the company (perhaps based on their title)
- The prospect's line of business
- Solutions/services applicable to the business
- Likely requirements and challenges of the business

Having this information readily available will lead to a productive discussion instead of the typical push and shove of a cold call. One way to make a connection with your prospect is to talk about referenceable companies. Companies are always interested in keeping track of what competitors are doing. Nationwide Insurance, for example, would be more interested in MetLife's business practices rather than Kroger's.

Be sure to pay attention when the prospect provides specifics on how to engage with its company; otherwise you may create resistance where there wasn't any. I once spoke with the CIO of a large company who was genuinely interested in bringing our client on board. His company was going to make some big changes in its retail systems and my client would be able to participate as a vendor. The prospect told me that he would be prepared to put a meeting together after he finished wrapping up some current projects. There would be no way that he could give attention to the matter for another three weeks. We suggested an earlier engagement, but it just wasn't possible, considering his workload.

We briefed our client on the conversation with the prospect, including his three-week timeframe. However, one of the client's internal sales reps actually called the guy two days later thinking they would push it, totally disregarding the request that the CIO had made. The CIO was annoyed, which was a logical response. The rep was disappointed that the CIO and company wouldn't talk with him and blamed us, but what did the rep expect? The CIO was clear about how this rep was to engage with him and had already committed to bringing my client in the deal.

Listen carefully to what prospects tell you. Make sure you understand their needs regarding the progress of your dialogue and then stay in alignment with their expectations.

Do you pay close attention to information you have about a prospect's needs and wishes?

21 Just Pick Up the Phone

An idle phone doesn't find opportunity.

You have to start somewhere. Begin by just picking up the phone. Don't allow yourself to focus on the challenges of cold calling so much that you procrastinate on picking up the phone.

You will certainly get rejected. You will make some mistakes. Prospects will ask you questions that you can't answer. Instead of letting things like that become a conversation-stopper, turn it to your advantage. Rather than ending the call, you could ask the prospect about the question. Asking questions such as, "Why do you ask?" or "What is the context around that question?" can give you further insight into the customer's requirements.

The more you call, the easier it gets. And once you get going, you'll find it really isn't so bad when you have the methods and tools to get the best results. Much of the apprehension about calling is based on things that haven't even happened. Thoughts like, "What if they hang up," "What if they ask me something I can't answer," or "What if I make a mistake" can make calling seem daunting. However, the more fluent you are, the easier it gets and the more effective you will be.

Don't worry if people ask a lot of difficult questions. This is a good thing, because the questions mean that they are searching for information and they want to see if you have a workable solution. Questions mean interest; it's a good thing.

There are certain qualities—such as insincerity, lack of integrity, and poor phone presence—that can hurt your efforts more than not being able to answer questions. The good news is that you have control over these things. As an experienced salesperson, you have already worked hard to eliminate many of them.

If you are offering complex solutions/services to business executives, you may find that many executives themselves won't know the in-depth details about the technology or about the problems with their organization past a certain level. I have spoken with many executives who were new to their positions. At times, you might discover that you know more about their technology than they do.

The key is to just do it. It is only a conversation with another person. If you keep in mind the rules that can help you here—being real, being helpful, and keeping your customer's interests and concerns in the front of the conversation—you will do just fine.

What you'll find once you pick up the phone is that it's an incredibly effective way to connect with your prospects and can be a very positive experience if you apply the principles that work.

Part of the fear comes from feelings that your call is annoying. But remember, your prospects also make calls when they are selling their products and services. Calling is part of doing business; they expect to get calls. If you are starting on a new endeavor, one you may not have all the answers for, just digging in and picking up the phone will get you there quickly.

Even if you've been cold calling for years, you can eliminate any distaste for it by improving your methods. Once you get some positive experiences under your belt, you'll feel more positive in general.

Do you procrastinate in getting started?

22 Use Voicemail to Connect with Prospects

Use voicemail as another form of communication.

Voicemail is a useful tool. It helps you reach out to people you have not been able to contact in person. However, a small percentage of prospects will return their sales calls, so how can you use it to your benefit?

Some reps feel that, because prospects often do not call back, leaving a voicemail is a waste of time. But think of voicemail as a form of communication similar to email or text messages. Don't let the one-way aspect of voicemail keep you from exploiting its benefits. People do listen to voicemail, and you can use it to your advantage.

One advantage of voicemail is that it helps you let prospects know that you're attempting to reach them. You can also remind them of your company name and business, keeping it fresh in their minds along with the solutions that you want to discuss. It sets the connection in motion; your prospects might forward them to others in the company, who, in turn, save them for later, or they look up your company on the Internet, etc.

Prospects who don't return calls are, nevertheless, often considering what you have to offer. It's not unusual for a prospect, once you get them on the phone, to say something like, "I listened to your voicemail and looked at your website." It is also not unusual for prospects to be prepared to talk when you call because they've researched your company.

Remember that the ball is always in your court, and you must leave a compelling voicemail if you want a call back. I initially script and test my voicemails to avoid drawn-out or ineffective messages. It allows me to concentrate on the content that I know will work.

When crafting your voicemail message think about the prospect's time and attention span. The formula is:

- Introduce yourself.
- Give the name of your company.
- State your role in the company.
- Mention some referenceable customer names.
- Brief them on the purpose of your call.

You can test the effectiveness of your voicemail by using your voicemail script to call your own phone number and leave yourself a message. Listen carefully to it and then ask yourself the question, "Would you call you back?" You can test if you lose interest in it, if it is too long, if it is unclear, or it is otherwise awkward. Put yourself in your prospects' shoes—consider how they might respond to such a message if they don't know who you are or what your company does.

Testing your messages gives you the opportunity to fix any problems with wording, intonation, or style. Keep making changes until the answer to, "Would you call back?" becomes an unqualified *yes*.

If the number of callbacks you receive declines, do this exercise again, leaving yourself a message and then listening to it from the prospect's perspective. You may discover that you sometimes talk too long and take too much time in getting to the point.

Would *you* call you back?

23 Don't Let a Telephone Change Who You Are

How to make your phone presence a reflection of your live presence.

All of us have taken sales calls in which the person on the other end spoke in a voice that had an impersonal quality. In some cases, our irritation with the whole experience was so great that it overrode any interest we might have had in the offer the person was talking about.

I have worked with some salespeople who interviewed well. They were bright, engaging, and charming people, who did very well face-to-face but, put in a phone environment, they turned into different people. It's important not to let the phone alter your "in-person personality." Use the phone to extend your presence beyond the room you are sitting in, not as a barrier to your normal communication and presence.

During one training session with a client, the sales rep I was working with was practicing her outbound calling. When she reached the CIO from a large company, she began talking to him in an almost disconnected manner, as if reading the script was important but having an open dialogue was not. He really was trying to talk to her, but eventually he simply asked for information and ended the call.

The trainee was totally unprepared for the fact that she had the CIO on the other end of the line—one who was willing to talk to her. Rather than just being herself and having a conversation, it became a mission to get through the script and get answers to the questions.

I imagine that she felt the conversation was slipping out of her control because of the absence of visual feedback. Whatever the reason, her unwarranted need to "read" the discussion rather than be flexible caused her to completely lose the charm that she actually possessed.

The principle is to behave no differently on the phone than in face-to-face situations. If you are an engaging person when interacting directly with someone, you can still be engaging on the phone. Talk a little slower to compensate for the lack of visual communication. Use voice gestures. Whatever you do, do not permit the phone to alter your overall presence.

Visualize people as if they were standing right in front of you, and do everything you do in person. Imagine you are talking to a neighbor, a family member, or someone with whom you are completely comfortable. It even helps to have a focal point while you are talking; it will help you do on the phone what you do well face to face. This is an important aspect of your calling, because you aren't there in person to add the gestures and mannerisms that may cover nervousness. Do whatever you can to make a seamless transition from your face-to-face persona to the personality that you express over the phone.

You may have heard the saying, "Smile and Dial." If you smile when you meet a new person face to face, then do that on the phone. You'll see (and hear) the difference. If you use a lot of gestures in person, use them during your call. Just because the person on the other end of the line can't see you doesn't mean that you are not impacting the dynamic of the call. Don't get so focused on the fact you are calling a stranger that it affects your performance.

How would your conversations with prospects be different if you spoke as if you were face to face?

24 | Be Flexible

It doesn't always go the way you planned.

When you make a cold call, you'll run into a variety of people, topics, situations, responses, and personalities. This is what makes it interesting, and it is what requires you to adapt to what is going on at the other end of the call.

You have to think on your feet because you don't always know what turn the call will take. You may call into a company and ask for a C-level executive's name. What if they transfer you there before you know it and the executive picks up? What will you say? Or the person on the other end isn't so chatty, and you have to ask a lot of questions to get the same information your last prospect volunteered? You may get someone who is hostile, or someone who is friendly.

The key is to be flexible. Some companies are very rigid about giving out names, while others freely give out names, numbers, and even emails. I find that to be more of a cultural difference, but don't let what one company does make a rule for what another might do.

When calling into a large transportation company, we contacted its Director of Telecommunications and he put us on hold for a couple of minutes. Then he accidentally disconnected the call, so we called back. He apologized and put us back on hold. When he rejoined the call, he was very rushed but interested. He turned it into a conference call with his outsourced provider and set it up for us to pursue our business with that company. It was a great opportunity but definitely not the normal call.

Being prepared for change also helps you avoid missing an opportunity when it presents itself. Some people have called into an executive's office thinking they would get the admin, but they got the executive and then hung up; granted, that is pretty amateur, but it illustrates how unprepared they were for the unexpected.

If a company won't give you the information you want, how can you be flexible enough to get in there? Mentally note all the options you have. For example, you can reach out to an accessible contact within the company, like an executive who is a peer of your intended contact, or an admin in another business unit. Do you know how to work a voicemail system to learn the prompts to dial by name?

Maybe you had been looking for someone's email address, then decide to call them directly and the prospect picks up the phone. If that happens to you, don't let it surprise you. Just talk to that person. Don't lose the prospect in order to send them an email first. One way to break the ice is to mention you were going to send them something, and you were calling because [the purpose of your call.] It's that simple.

The point is to approach cold calling in ways that improve reach and effectiveness. Call into a company with the ability to adapt to how the company networks you, screens you, talks to you, refers you, or whatever else might happen.

The benefit to you is that you become more fluent, more confident, and much more effective in how you penetrate accounts. And you won't lock yourself into a smaller and smaller path due to incorrectly assuming the call has to be cut and dry.

Are you flexible with your approach?

25 Admins Are Not the Enemy

Administrative assistants can connect you with your buyer.

Some sales reps look at administrative assistants as gatekeepers, obstacles to be avoided in their quest for a sale. Some sales reps, in fact, try intimidation or condescension as their main tactic. Others think that it requires sneakiness or deception to successfully get past their roadblocks. However, your success lies not in evasive maneuvers but in straightforwardness.

The administrative assistant's job is to run interference for the boss, but not necessarily for someone else's boss. Depending on how you approach them, most admins do not mind "screening" you over to someone else. However, talking down to them never works. These people are a key part of the organization and play a big role in managing access to their bosses. They get paid very well to do that, and they earn every cent.

It pays (literally) to be nice to them, in a professional way. If you do that, these people can be your best friends in the company. They know a lot about the department and also may have a better contact for you. They have numbers and email addresses and also know who reports to whom. If you reach out to them properly, they may feel confident disclosing information, helping you reach your goal much faster. In fact, most of them want to be helpful to the people who treat them professionally. To get to the point that they are helping you with information, you can say something like this: "I have a quick question. Who is in charge of ...?" When you deal with them in a professional manner, it has been my experience that they can, and will, direct you to the person you really need.

Of course, you will meet some admins (and people in general) who are just not helpful. If you have to get around them, a couple of ways would be to ask the front desk for the extension of the person you are looking for, or you can ask to go directly to that person's voicemail. Many times, front-desk staff are happy to comply, and then you can leave a message for your prospect who can call you back.

Do you view admins as obstacles? Can you think of ways they can help you?

26 | Choose Your Words Carefully

This isn't about being polite or impolite. It is about handling your business at the level of your prospects. When cold calling, it is important to establish your peer status with the prospect. People won't disclose a lot of information to people who are not at their level. Your medium is the phone, and through it you must make sure that your prospects see you as a colleague, an advisor, and someone "like them." The good news is that you have control over that perception.

You must work at your executive presence in your calling. Always think of yourself as speaking to your peers. There is no need to "put on airs," nor should you "talk up" to the person on the other end of the line. Calling people in a business environment Mr. or Mrs. is less common than it once was. You don't need to do that. You don't have to ask permission to talk to them. Executives don't apologize to each other for calling. They aren't going to call one of their peers and open the discussion with an apology and ask permission to speak. They just start talking, which is what you need to do. You are creating a mental picture in the prospect's head of who you are, and you want that picture to be as credible as possible. The information you are bringing to prospects should be perceived as coming from a professional, someone they can trust. Someone "like them."

To do this well, you must think about the conversation before you have it. You should lay out what you want to say so that you can be natural, prepare for contingencies, stay focused, and put the best message forward. Practicing your call beforehand, in order to be natural, may seem to be a paradox, but it really isn't. Much of what makes you sound rehearsed is the nervousness and the lack of a plan for guiding the conversation.

Think about current industry terms and buzzwords; do you know them? Are you still using terminology that went out with Windows 3.1? Think about this, because it's important to be deliberate with the words you use.

Record yourself as if you were talking with a prospect. Then listen to your recording objectively and make any adjustments. As a rule, don't end your sentences with a question in your voice; say everything with confidence in an even tone. Watch your volume so that you don't fade off, which also will give you a soft presence that you don't want.

Just recently, I got a call from Rachelle, the rep at InsideView. She worked hard to connect with me and to attain her goal of putting a meeting on the calendar. The thing that stood out was that she knew I was busy and respected that, but she didn't put herself in a position where I would think of her as a nuisance. She didn't misuse words and terms that decreased her credibility, which would have made me want to avoid her calls.

Speak as an equal. As part of your preparation, take the time to understand not only buzzwords in your industry but also the industries you are targeting. Your choice of words is part of your presence, so use them to make yourself more effective.

Think about who has influenced you the most. It is likely those who were relaxed, confident, and assuring. Those who have turned you off, no doubt, were anxious, overbearing, or lacking some quality that builds trust. You don't want to get lumped in with the rest of the calls your prospects reject. Instead, go in there armed with what you need to build credibility.

Do you think about the words you use? Are you careful with your phone presence?

27 Don't Do All the Talking

Listening is more than half of selling.

One of the major errors cold callers make is to feel that they have to do all of the talking. Many times this occurs because the sales rep feels that he has to get the words out before the prospect can say no. However, the prospect is then turned off because the presentation did not address the prospect's specific issue.

I remember an instance in which an AT&T business phone systems representative called me on the phone. He gave me a long spiel about all of his products. He really pushed for me to make an appointment to talk about a particular phone solution, but under the best of circumstances I wouldn't use that product. The problem was that he never asked me what I needed, which could have been another product he offered. The main theme of the call was me telling him it wouldn't make sense, and him telling me it would. No sale.

It is more important to ask your prospect questions early. Your goal is to explore the ways you can solve problems for prospects. However, if you don't ask questions, how will you know what you can offer? How will you know where to direct your focus if you don't ask about their problems?

In the initial discussions, you should be talking very little about your solutions. Your concern about making a sale may cause you to do otherwise, but keep the conversation mainly about *their* businesses—not yours. Your goal is to identify their needs (if any). If they have some specific areas to talk about, you will want to write them down, so that when you do speak of your solutions, you speak in terms of their problems and how your solutions can address them. If they don't have any current needs, then keep the information you've collected, as it may be useful in the future. Business environments and challenges change rapidly, so you can reach back out to them when circumstances change down the road.

A good formula for your conversations is this:

- Introduce yourself. Don't use a title in that introduction, especially if "sales" is in your title—it can be a turn off sometimes.
- State what your company does, and for whom. It is not necessary to go into extreme detail; think two sentences.

Start asking questions. Review Rule 10 on asking good questions. It doesn't have to be a question that puts the prospect on the spot, but something you can use to find common ground to build on.

By limiting your talk time up front, you'll have a better idea of how to move the discussion forward and talk about what counts. If you are doing all the talking, you risk saying something about which the prospect has no interest, missing what the prospect is interested in, and consequently not speaking effectively to the prospect's requirement.

When talking to a prospect, you are on a fact-finding mission. You can't get at those facts if you are doing all the talking.

Can you listen more to your prospects?

28 Quit Trying to "Sell" on a Cold Call

A complex sale takes time to develop.

You don't want to create sales resistance on your first call. However, the typical cold calling mentality focuses on closing the deal from the outset. While closing a sale is the ultimate goal, single-mindedly pursuing a close causes you to come off as a hard sell.

I recently took a call from a company that does marketing events. I had a discussion with the "biz dev guy" who was really trying hard to close me on the idea, but it wasn't something that made sense for me at the time. He wanted to schedule a meeting, which wasn't necessary. I suggested that he call me the following quarter, but he wanted to schedule a meeting for that time as well. It was clear that he was paid by the number of meetings, but do you want to be that obvious to your prospects?

Many sales reps make calls with the wrong elements in mind: the size of the prospect's budget, whether they are talking to a decision-maker (and if this person is closeable), how big the opportunity could be, and the estimated timeline. None of these things, however, takes into account the customer's perspective. That is why most people dislike salespeople initially. They don't see them as helpful and instead see them as overbearing and trying to make them do something they don't want to do, hence the sales resistance.

Think about an encounter with a hard sell and how you felt about it. Have you ever avoided a car dealer because you knew the salespeople were all about getting you to buy as soon as you stepped on the lot? This may be the same vibe you are projecting to your prospects. From the outset, it is better to think about: how you can help this prospect, what they need, who they are, what they do, and the appropriate next steps. By the way, it isn't always a meeting. This thought process will change the nature of your call from a hard-sell with a lot of resistance, to a collaborative effort in which you are building a new business relationship.

As you proceed through the call, you may determine that you just can't help the prospect at this time. The prospect's problem doesn't match your solution, or the prospect is simply not in the market for a solution right now.

However, there is much you can learn from these conversations. Remember, you are not selling; rather, you are building a relationship. You have still learned a lot about the prospect and the prospect's business and should have documented it in your notes. You can still contact this prospect again later by phone or email. It may not be as easy to win this account as others, but you have the information to move it forward. One thing is clear: if you had pushed too hard for just a meeting or a close, your prospect may have gone quiet and discontinued the dialogue.

Your strategy in cold calling should be to take the focus off yourself and put it on the prospect—where it belongs.

Do you need to find ways to soften your approach?

29 Use Gestures

Animation in a presentation can be vocal rather than visual.

A classic 1971 study by UCLA psychologist Albert Mehrabian showed that when audience members were asked what they remembered about a speaker from a verbal, vocal, and visual standpoint, they indicated just seven percent of their recall was verbal (what was said); 38 percent of their recall was vocal (how it was said); and 55 percent was visual (the speaker's body language and confidence). When you are on the phone, you don't have the 55 percent that is visual. However, you can use the other 38 percent of vocal communication to attain success.

The phone shouldn't change the way you communicate. If you naturally gesture when talking, then do it while you are on the phone. This helps you to maintain your natural presence. You may not believe it, but your prospect can hear the difference. There are other differences in phone conversations that you should be aware of that will help you.

Pauses over the phone are more exaggerated than in person. When you are in person, even though no one is speaking, there is still a lot of body language communication, and pauses don't seem to be so long. On the phone, though, a pause seems like forever. Don't feel that you have to fill those pauses, because the conversation will come off as rushed or awkward. This is especially true if you are at a point in the conversation where you are asking questions regarding purchase of your product or service. In person, you would allow that pause, to give the prospect time to think. It is the same in a phone conversation. Let the prospect have that time.

Train your voice to remain level throughout the conversation. Don't exaggerate mannerisms, which can sound strange and can detract from your conversation. This can happen sometimes when you get nervous or don't feel prepared. Some people tend to turn everything into a question by increasing intonation at the end of their sentences, because they don't have visual feedback to help them pace the conversation properly. You can remedy this by assuming that you have positive visual feedback during your conversation. I have found it helpful to use a mirror. This way you can catch the things you do on the phone that you don't do in person and vice versa.

Visualize that you are speaking to the prospect in person. Talk to prospects as though they are sitting across the desk from you. Also, when you are making your introductions by phone, it should sound just like your in-person intros. See yourself shaking their hands as you talk to them.

The most important thing to change when you're on the phone is to speak much more slowly. Many people talk much faster in person. But in person, there is the non-verbal element to facilitate comprehension. You don't have that feedback in a phone conversation, so you have to slow it down, which takes getting used to. You should gesture with your voice but not by changing the pitch so that it sounds awkward or sing-songy. Instead, incorporate the natural things you do in person into your phone conversations. Your prospects will respond to the difference. After all, you can tell the difference between a conversation in which you were engaged and one that bored you. The difference is that the excitement and positive feelings came through in one conversation, whereas the lack of enthusiasm was conveyed loudly and clearly in the other.

Do you use your normal gestures when you talk on the phone?

30 How to Troubleshoot Your Calling

Accurate diagnosis leads to improvement.

When things aren't going as well as you expect, you need to know how to fix them. How do you figure out why you aren't getting results?

You have to determine where your process is breaking down. The problem may be that when you get a prospect on the phone, you have good conversations; however, you don't get return calls when you leave messages. Perhaps there is something wrong with the voicemails you leave. Are they too long? Are they too fast? Does the prospect understand what you are talking about? Did you reach out to the wrong contact?

As you consider these questions, leave yourself a voicemail. After you listen to it, ask yourself if you would return that call. Most prospects will not respond to a message (voicemail or email) that is unclear. They are too busy to call you back to try to figure it out or send you to the right person. You can also ask your prospects about your message during the next contact: "Did you get my voicemail? Did it make sense?" Note the answer mentally; it provides great feedback.

Are you getting shut down by administrative assistants when you call? Then something may be wrong with your approach. I was once training someone in the cold calling process. Everyone this person talked with seemed to be asking for more information, but no one was connecting her to the prospects. We looked at her process. As it turned out, she was giving way too much information to the admin during her calls. The admins generally had no idea what the caller was talking about. So, their response was to ask her to send them more information. Because they didn't understand what the trainee was looking for, they would not refer her to anyone else. The solution was to use the admin as a springboard by asking, "I have a quick question, can you tell me who…?" She no longer over informed the admins she reached with a full overview of her intent. This resulted in fewer requests to send more information, and more connections to desired prospects.

If you are getting cut off early in the discussion with your prospects, analyze your process. What does your intro look like? Can you think of any reasons why your customer would not be interested in pursuing the conversation further? Are you perhaps saying things at the beginning of the call that aren't really relevant, causing the prospect to think their time is being wasted? Are you talking to the right person?

Troubleshooting early will keep you from wasting calls that could otherwise be productive. Look at your results now. Are you satisfied? If not, maybe there is a glitch in your process that you can address. You can always drill down to the problem area causing the call to break down.

Breakdown signs include:

- A networking process that isn't working
- Voicemail messages aren't getting results
- Admins screen you or won't give you information
- Calls are often cut off early
- Lack of progress during calls
- Refusal to disclose information
- Requests for you to send information before speaking further

Change the content of your discussion. If people are refusing information or a next step, maybe they are not sure what you are talking about or feel pushed. If they ask for information first, maybe you need to just say okay and then continue the discussion. Your calls should be more of a discovery-by-chance type of feeling; if they are pushing back on you, could it be they feel they are being "telemarketed?" Think of the area of breakdown, which will tell you where the problem lies.

Cold calling is a predictable activity that you can fine tune. Take the time to stand back and look at what your problem areas may be; once you fix them, your results will change dramatically.

Is there an area you need to troubleshoot?

31 Learn as You Go

Regard every call you make as a source of learning and experience.

Your goal is to learn something from each and every call and to build on that knowledge. Your knowledge base is in a process of constant improvement and growth. With each conversation, you gain invaluable details that apply to various industries, and you learn how to gauge the business executives' view, depending on their roles. All of this will affect your ability to have productive discussions with your prospects about your offer.

I was once working with a company that had a hub solution for enterprise data conversions. During our calls to various industries, many different pain points surfaced that were unique to the customer industry. One of those points was identified during a lengthy discussion with a restaurant chain that was having problems with accepting data formats from their liquor distributors. It was a major issue in its industry and one of which our client was unaware. We were able to reuse what we learned from the restaurant chain in other calls by asking if other prospects had similar problems. As a result, we gained many follow-up opportunities. The key was using existing knowledge, rather than starting the next call from zero.

As you gain expertise about your prospects' environments, use it to improve your future conversations. This is going to be a huge part of your own training. Much of your fluency on certain subjects will come from speaking directly with prospects, and then reusing that information on subsequent calls.

Work on seeing the big picture as you progress through your calls. Look at all of the information you have gathered in your discussions over time. What can you reuse that will help with future calls? You have the ability to correlate the business intelligence you've gathered from previous calls and use it to improve subsequent calls. Use that broad knowledge base to your advantage to aid your prospects in better communicating their needs.

Sometimes I see that people are not really absorbing and reusing the information prospects provide. Their calls tend to start and stay the same over time, not reflecting everything they should have learned from talking with dozens of people. Use the rich content you have in your head to make your calls more informative, both in the questions you ask and in the information you provide.

If you find you aren't progressing as you'd like, step back and think about the things your prospects disclose to you. There is probably a lot more information you have been exposed to than you realize. If you learn something new from prospects regarding their views of their requirements, do you now use that to probe for something similar in other companies' requirements?

The point is to listen and absorb, and then turn around and reuse that information to have richer conversations as you proceed in your calls.

How much have you learned from your customers? Can you see the big picture as your customers see it?

Connect the Dots

Find ways to bring it all together in the discussion.

Solutions have a powerful impact throughout a company. Whether it is a financial services solution or a technology solution, it is important to recognize that your product touches many areas of a business or even other organizations. This extended reach represents many potential prospects. Getting in front of prospects is what builds your business. As you consider your solutions or services, do you understand how you can call into different areas of the business?

I have a long-term client, a broadband access provider. Its main focus is satellite data networks. When it goes into a company, we have to consider all areas of the business that may be involved, including marketing, human resources, training, and supply chain, so that we can present a comprehensive solution to that customer. Each of these departments would be impacted by a large-scale implementation of a newer data network and related services. Understanding those requirements helps us speak to the actual business requirements my client can solve. Understanding the innerworkings of the company can help us penetrate the account more effectively.

Look at the business as a big map. You can then overlay your solution onto the business map and view each impacted area as a possible strategic entry point. Use this map view to call into multiple areas in the account regarding specific topics. Each contact is an opportunity to learn more about the company and to attain two things: entry into the account and a 360-degree view of your prospect.

The nice thing about doing this over the phone is that you can reach out to numerous areas within the company very quickly and gain traction with your prospects much faster than would otherwise be possible. It is definitely worth taking the time to understand the various areas of your prospect companies.

If you are having a hard time grasping this method, here are some helpful questions:

- Does the operations department make decisions that drive the use of your product?
- Do departmental requirements affect the vendor choice? What are those? Who should you talk to?
- Are there areas of the business that suffer from not having a remedy for the problem? What kinds of questions do you need to ask to find out?
- Can you reach out directly to the purchasing department and see how it brings in a vendor?
- Does a manager view the requirement differently than a Vice President does?
- Is there a back door way to get into the account? Maybe there is a group that would benefit from your solution that has influence with the actual buyer.

You'll find it interesting and effective to know all the areas of a business and understand all the touch points for a particular offer. You'll also start seeing your results increase because now you have opened many doors instead maintaining a narrow focus on a single person or group.

Do you know the map of your prospects? What does it look like?

33 Understand Your Customer

Be able to speak with authority about your prospect's business and needs.

It is extremely important that you, as a sales professional, know the various areas of the business and industry before you call into an account. It is important to connect the dots, ask questions, and build your domain expertise as you progress through your campaigns. There is also the aspect of showing insight when you reach out to a prospect, bearing in mind the specific issues of each prospect.

Before you pick up the phone, make sure you have a clear understanding of what the company does. For example, consider a financial services company. Some of its needs may include security, high availability, network infrastructure, procurement interface (purchasing), sourcing, engineering, customer data (CRM), and sales. Actually, these areas could apply to most business types. The key is to build a comprehensive list of the various parts of its business.

As you consider this list and your solutions, what are the strengths you can highlight in view of a company's needs? Consider the relevance of your suite of solutions and services to a particular industry. Then you can examine your customer base for similar issues and relevant solutions to apply to those issues. Geoffrey Moore, in his book, *Crossing the Chasm*, talks about the concept of creating "a pragmatist customer base that is referenceable," to "provide us access to other mainstream prospects," since pragmatists use references in their buying decisions. When you provide solutions for your customers, make sure you can show the value you brought to them, because it could lead to exposure with other potential customers who will use that experience to make their buying decisions.

Plan your entry to an account. You are cold calling, so you have only a short window to get prospects' attention. Speak to each prospect based on his or her particular business issues and offer relevant examples. Leverage your experience in dealing with common industry problems. You should be familiar with basic industry lingo, regardless of the industry; however, this requires preparation, so plan in advance how you'll approach the account.

It takes only a few minutes, but preparation can be a catalyst to get your prospect to the "tell me more" stage. I have seen reps who are looking only for that "low hanging fruit," and they miss a lot of opportunities by saying the wrong thing and losing their prospect's interest unnecessarily. It will greatly benefit you to speak to your prospects based on their businesses and not confine yourself to a one-size-fits-all approach.

Some things you can do to show you know your customers:

- Pull together a list of similar client names to reference and group them.
- Consider the practices specific to their businesses.
- Plan the introduction of your service/product based on their industries.

How much do you know about your customer?

34 Have Fun

Be serious about your work but have a good time.

Do you actually enjoy doing what you are doing? It makes all the difference if you do.

Cold calling exposes you to new people and situations, as does the sales field in general. Long-term relationships are the desired result. If you root out the things that cause cold calling to become a chore, you can have a really good time with it. Building your skills actually helps you enjoy your work, because it becomes less of a push-pull struggle and more of a path toward opportunity for you and a key to solving problems for your clients. As you develop more skill, you can approach people without fear or worry about the "what ifs." You start to really understand your customers and have some meaningful discussions. The process starts to become more of a science than an art, with predictable results.

More than twenty years ago, I was brainstorming with a colleague of mine about sales slumps. The conclusion we reached was that the harder we tried, the worse it got. In part, this was due to the unconscious signals of desperation that came through in our voices when we were under pressure, and the ensuing shift in focus. So we did an experiment. Our goal was to *not* care what happened when we called. I mean really not care, even to the point where we were slightly put off that we had to write up an order and keep talking. And it worked. Not because we were manipulating the conversation, but because we took the pressure off ourselves by only talking about the requirement and knowing we were helping clients get something *they* wanted. We saw that they felt great about buying our products and realized our role in the process.

This was long before Solution Selling and other sales methodologies that manage the actual buying cycle. Doing this made the calls fun again, and it wasn't about us, but about the dialogue. And to this day, I never worry about the end result, but I am totally committed to helping clients get what they need. The scripts I write for clients are not pushing for appointments, but they are actually meant to assess the potential for further discussions. It's all about the solution and how to explore what will provide the best fit.

Think of what you enjoy about cold calling. How much do you know about your industry from all the conversations you've had? Do you view the call to your prospect as a break from what they were doing? That is totally reasonable, as their day may be filled with mundane work and stressful moments, and your call can actually break up the monotony. They might be able to solve a big problem—and you gave them a chance to articulate it. It's a good thing.

I like to know what's going on in the various industries and businesses I deal with. It fuels my aptitude and, in turn, makes helping customers enjoyable. I get to exercise "big picture" thinking. As my knowledge broadens, I find it easier to eliminate the negatives, which means I get to fully experience and savor the success I have achieved.

In another rule, I mention the importance of your attitude; this is something you can control, and it has a huge impact on your first call of the day if you look forward to it.

Do you have a good time with what you do?

35 Use Resources Wisely

Make your job easier through modern technology.

Cold calling is a relative term in 2008. Twenty-five years ago, calls were truly cold calls. We didn't have the Internet to search press releases, contact names, or financial, competitor, and other pertinent business data. I remember when I was about eighteen years old, and I called a company that had a man's name, something like the Frank Smith Company or whatever it was. I thought I was being smart starting at the top, so I asked for Frank Smith. I was informed that he had died forty years earlier! That wouldn't happen today, because now there are numerous services and research tools available. Use these tools to your advantage, and they can make your cold call *not so cold*.

Below are some popular sources that many sales organizations use in their operation:

Hoovers provides in-depth company information (http://www.hoovers.com).

Genius (http://www.genius.com) allows you to look at your customer's behavior and responses regarding individual or multi-contact email campaigns. They are another partner of The Vanella Group, Inc., and we recommend them to clients so they can see if their prospects are looking at the emails they have sent. Honestly, if someone takes the time to click on your link and look through your site, it's worth a call.

Jigsaw (http://www.jigsaw.com) is one of The Vanella Group, Inc. partners. This company has done a great job putting together a database with contact info of prospects within companies. It will put you in the right direction to call around and find the appropriate contact person.

LinkedIn (http://www.linkedin.com) is a social networking site. You can find contacts in an account or background on prospects you are trying to reach. You may know people already in your prospect companies.

OneSource (http://www.onesource.com) provides information on companies, down to the organization level. On this site, you can even find info on executive turnover, tenure, and data you can use to build a picture of the target organization.

Inside View (http://www.insideview.com) aggregates information from multiple sources on companies that are found on the Web.

LinkSiliconValley (http://www.linksiliconvalley.com) is a site that provides detailed information on the Silicon Valley startup community. This site is integrated with other social network sites.

SalesForce.com (http://www.salesforce.com) is a web-based CRM tool. The Vanella Group, Inc. is a Salesforce partner and many of our clients use it successfully.

Google and Yahoo Business (http://finance.google.com and http://business.yahoo.com) allow you to find information on businesses and companies in targeted searches. In addition, you can search Google and Yahoo to get all of the information related to a company or business that is currently on the Web.

Don't make your calls colder than they already are. Spend a few extra minutes and get some background on your prospect so you can make the most effective progress with your calls.

Are you familiar with these tools? Will you use them to your advantage?

People Like to Help

People want to help you, so don't miss the opportunity.

Think about the times that people have called you asking for your help with a topic or question. Did you mind helping them? If you are like most people, you really didn't mind it at all. In fact, you may even have been glad to do it. Your prospects are like that, too, so don't miss that point by expecting them to be hostile towards your call.

A lot of sales reps go for "the kill" in their initial sales calls. Years ago, one of my client's reps made a remark that when he looks at a lead, he thinks, "Can I make the kill?" Unfortunately, his thinking was short term, and he missed a lot of really good opportunities because he had a cynical way of looking at his prospects. People who think like that only want to hit the target; but with that type of focus, they never think about the prospect as a potential peer or a resource, only as a deal. Consequently, they tend to end up with neither.

Obviously, a salesperson wants to make a sale; however, when the call reeks of a sales agenda and lacks substance, it will generally be dumped into the "vendor line." The vendor line is the bureaucratic process that companies set up to manage the evaluation of potential vendors. When people tell me they often get dumped in the vendor line, it tells me they aren't asking for information the right way.

If you find yourself in this situation, change your approach, and you will change your results. For example, you might approach the initial call by saying something like, "I was hoping you could help me out," or "I had a quick question." When you put it this way, the person will usually pause and ask how he or she can help you. You can then simply ask, "Can you tell me, who does [the function you need to contact]?"

If you reach the wrong person or are not sure to whom you need to speak, why not just ask for help? There is a difference between making a simple request for information and being pushy. When you say, "I'm with such and such company, and I need to know who does this," you're more likely to get screened. The best approach is to ask a quick question, don't put a lot of information around it, and appeal to people's natural willingness to help. Even if they say they don't know the specific information you requested, ask if there is another way they can help.

When considering the sales call from the prospect company's perspective, it is obvious that, initially, they receive mostly qualifying questions. When a sales rep calls and rushes into questions that will indicate their chances of making the sale, those calls tend to be more abrupt and will be screened. When the salesperson doesn't think the prospect will be productive, then they just as abruptly drop the conversation. This approach will be distasteful to the prospect and will inevitably diminish the caller's chance at success.

Stand out as different. Rather than assuming the prospect can't do anything for you, and in turn, taking a "burn the bridge" approach, just take the initiative and ask if they can help.

With all of the rude, short, apathetic calls that business people receive, most will respond to someone who just says "Hey, can you help me? I wanted to ask a quick question: who's the person who does.....?" Before you know it, you have what you need. You can even ask, "Do you have the number handy by chance?" You'll be surprised how helpful people are, and it's great when you take the resistance out of it and let people help you move around within the account.

Are you letting the people on the other end help you get what you need?

37 How to Avoid the Vendor Line

Stand out from the crowd.

Most companies have a formal process for screening and managing vendors. They determine whether they want to do business with you based on the information you supply. The net result is that you will eventually end up in their voicemail system, otherwise known as the "vendor line." This process is usually deferred to a common department that really doesn't know what you do. The bad thing about it is that most deals don't happen in the vendor line.

How do you stay out of this line? You want to talk to the particular person with the business problem or someone who can get you to that person, not the department administering the vendor line or the front desk. However, some companies screen everyone, no matter what. If this is the case, it will require a little creativity to stand out and avoid staying in the vendor line.

You can navigate most companies with patience and a big-picture perspective. Identify someone (not necessarily your target) in the company who can provide a bridge to the person you need to contact. You may be looking for the person in charge of financial reporting to the Securities and Exchange Commission (SEC) in a large company. You must get to the right area, floor, or department. Find someone in finance, and then simply ask for help. A straightforward, "Can you help me? Who's the person in your group that does the SEC reporting?" can open the door. Don't over-inform. If you don't get directly to your contact, get to an executive who may know the person you need to speak with. Don't hesitate to ask their admin for the information you need, just do it fast without a lot of pomp.

If you are calling the front desk, focus on getting to the right area or peer group for your contact. This means you need to do some homework on the company before you start calling, so you know how to reach the person you need, under any circumstances that may arise to complicate the call. As an example, perhaps you have a supply chain solution and are working to find someone in the supply chain group. So you call into the company and say, "Hey, I have a quick question, who's the VP of Supply Chain?" (quickly, with no pomp). If they don't know and start asking about the "nature of your call," say you had a question to ask about some of the planning then quickly ask for another contact: "Okay, transfer me to Joan Williams, please." Don't overcomplicate it, or you may be screened.

You can call similar departments and ask them for assistance. If you are trying to reach CIOs (most are difficult to reach in large companies), ask for their admins. The point is, don't think linearly, as though navigation in a company must be in a straight line. That way, you avoid getting stalled at the entry points where they screen you and dump you in the vendor line.

Be prepared:

* Know who you want to reach.
* Consider alternate contacts.
* Talk to admins who might know to whom you could be transferred.

If you get dumped in the vendor line before you realize it, just wait a while and call back and ask to speak with a contact you already know. Once you get past the front desk or the department admin, you usually are out of the weeds of the vendor line.

Can you find more than one path to your contacts?

Rule

38 Follow Up with Email

Don't underestimate the effectiveness of email.

Your main purpose in calling your prospect is to engage in discussions that will eventually lead to a deal. In business, email is an invaluable tool and should be used in conjunction with your calling. In the sales process, once a prospect or an opportunity is identified, sending an email with information is often the next step. Also, if you are having difficulty reaching a prospect via phone, try emailing them instead; many people are more receptive to email. Because it is an extension of your calling presence, you must also pay attention to how you construct your email communication.

You want to maintain control of the dialogue in your emails, so be succinct. The phone is your main channel and it should coordinate with your ancillary channels, like email and voicemail. As such, you do not need to add extraneous information in your emails. Use email to reach those prospects that you can't reach by phone. You can use voicemail to let them know who you are and that you're trying to reach them. These all work in concert to initiate the discussion. I have also found that some executives are actually more responsive to email than voicemail. That being said, be certain that your email communication is clear, brief, and relevant.

When you craft your first email to the prospect, instead of using a formal introduction, why not write as if you were on the phone? I have found this approach to be extremely effective:

> Hi Vicki,
>
> "I thought it would be easier to reach your via email. I left a voicemail for you the other day, I don't know if you got a chance to get to it yet. [Lets them off the hook for blowing off your voicemails.]
>
> I was hoping to speak with you briefly about.....
>
> You may know we work with... [Cite big customers they would relate to] in the area of [what you do]...."

In the opening paragraphs, there is no need to describe yourself, talk about your title, or add anything irrelevant. Just write what you need to say. As in a live conversation, don't say too much about you, but rather, focus on their potential (or known) needs and how you can best help them. Be brief.

The best emails are concise. As you craft your email, don't assume that there is a closed deal ahead. I once read a rep's follow-up email, dealing with a prospect that mentioned they had a tight budget. The sales rep discussed financing options and other details about the deal—but he hadn't yet spoken with the prospect. Don't let email create resistance. Use it to increase their interest.

Your prospect won't read that much information, because prospects probably get 150+ emails a day. You have the same short window in email as you do on the phone, so get to the point. The minute they come across something in your email they don't understand or feel they don't want, they will lose interest.

Use email as a tool to create and develop interest, but not to say what you can say in person or on the phone. Anything about a prospect's specific requirements should be said on the phone or in a meeting. If a prospect comes back and asks for specifics, use that to cite brief examples, and tell them you need to know more to give them the right information.

You can get a very decent response to email as part of your cold calling efforts. When you have it, use it.

Do you use email to broaden your reach?

39 Don't Focus on a Single Contact

You want to use a network of contacts to identify an opportunity.

When reaching out to a company, there are numerous contacts that can help develop the account, if you know how and where to look. To be successful, you have to think in three dimensions: up, across, and down the organization. Many salespeople tend to focus on only one main contact. This is perhaps someone who helped them in the past, or it is the first name they were given as the corporate contact, or it is simply the person who seems to be an appropriate contact. The problem is that when that contact is lost or doesn't work out, then the account fails to progress further. The solution is to reach out to numerous contacts at the start.

You may find yourself trying to reach the CFO of a company. A good strategy is to call the Vice President of Operations, or the Vice President of Finance, or IT. Calling these other executives broadens your reach within the company, and they can help you, because their roles tend to touch on or directly involve what you may be offering. You want to cover as many bases as possible in order to make headway with the account. You do not want to stall your progress just because you can't get to the CFO directly. The requirements you are looking for may not roll up to just one person.

Let's say you sell an application lifecycle management solution. You want to talk to the VP of Application Development. Is there a way you could also frame a message around ROI that is applicable to the finance department or the VP of Quality Assurance or some other executive? In your research, have you found directors or other senior management with whom you could speak in order to gain access to the account? Are there peer executives who can help influence the decision? The key here is to marshal resources that will help you speed up the process. Don't focus your efforts on one person as your prospect.

When coaching someone on cold calling, one of the first things I do is analyze the contact database. Oftentimes, I will see numerous calls to just one person, someone who is usually non-responsive. In that situation, I help the trainee find other contacts that can help him or her gain another entry-point. When they speak with someone else, the sales rep realizes that the first person they tried to contact didn't have the job they had assumed, which explained that contact's unresponsiveness.

You should not wait until you have a high number of calls into an account before you make use of additional resources. Instead, make it a part of your lead management process to reach out to a few people and leave messages; someone will call you back and help you find the correct contact person. Doing this regularly can do more than jumpstart a stalled account; it can also increase your penetration into a larger group of accounts simultaneously.

Have you checked your contacts today?

40 Refresh Your Database

Set limits on how much you work in a single account.

If you find that your production is decreasing, examine your contact database. The problem could be that your accounts are exhausted, meaning that you have too many calls into accounts with no productivity or too many accounts for which you can't reach the right contact. Some accounts might even be experiencing an internal issue into which you have no visibility, such as an acquisition or merger, which is causing the lack of response. For now, you can't proceed with them, so focus on new accounts and revisit the others later. Refreshing the account base you are working on makes a huge difference in productivity.

As you stage the accounts you want to call, be mindful of certain things. Be careful of calling on too many accounts at one time. Decide on a number that you can thoroughly handle at once. Maybe it's twenty, maybe forty; whatever it is, don't overload yourself. If you do, you won't be able to gain momentum with the accounts because you won't be able to devote enough time to each one. Remember, the vast amount of your cold calling success is found in reaching people at their desks, and it takes a concerted effort to do that. If you are spread too thin, you won't see the volume of opportunities.

Your focus should be on managing your territory in a systematic way to ensure proper coverage. One method I find most effective is to segment your accounts; then pull one group—based on any factor you choose—and focus on that group only. Of course, how you implement this method will depend on your sales environment.

CRM (customer relationship management) and SFA (sales force automation) tools are excellent for managing your sales territory. I find it useful to pull a subset of your territory or accounts regularly, whether daily or weekly. In this process, you may have to retire some accounts for which there are a high number of non-responsive calls. There is some art to this, and you will have to determine what makes sense, but the point is that this should be built into your regular sales management process.

If I see someone whose production is falling, this is one of the things I consider. And typically, I find an exhausted list of accounts. Another point to remember: You don't want to manage your database on a large scale, introducing and dumping large numbers of accounts. You can add accounts incrementally to augment those you cycle out. So if you talk to ten accounts this week, pull ten new ones to add in your list.

Evaluate your account list. If you see that you have put in a large number of calls, reached out to multiple contacts, and sent the emails, but aren't getting responses, do a little research on the account. You may find that there is a major event or issue in that company (restructure, new offering, or merger). In that case, make a note and just let the account rest for awhile. Then you can go back to the database and add some fresh contacts into the mix.

Keeping a fresh list ensures you'll have a combination of accounts, some that take a few calls and some that require more effort. You'll see a more predictable level of results if you manage yourself at this level.

Have you refreshed your contact database lately? Is it a regular part of your account management strategy?

41

Be Aware of the Facets of Your Work

Sales is a skilled profession, so treat it as such.

As a sales professional, beginning or experienced, you already know that there are many areas to monitor as you call on accounts. There is way more to it than just numbers and phone calls. You have to be aware of the way you perceive your role, the way you think about yourself and your prospects, and the various ways you communicate with others. You have to manage how many accounts you call, what industries the accounts are in, as well as how you "fit" with their business.

Your job is directly impacted by how much you know about your prospects and how well you can sit in their seats. Do you focus on solving their problems and resolving their challenges? Do you know the point pain topics to bring up with them?

Are you leveraging all possible areas to engage with your clients? Are you having the rich discussions you need to have by using all the industry information you have in your head and at your fingertips?

It sounds like a lot, and it can be. However, paying attention to these things will increase your results and put you way ahead of others in your line of business. Cold calling is not something to dread. Use this knowledge to tweak it here and adjust it there, and you will find you can dramatically change your results. This is how you will open doors for yourself.

While your work has many facets, over time it will become second nature and you won't have to put so much thought into these areas. Cold calling is really just an extension of what you do in person every day: meet people. But it takes deliberate effort and skill to make it count. You have a limited window of availability, so you have to control what happens as much as you can on your end.

These rules may not all apply to you, but I'm sure there are some areas in which you can do some self-examination and make improvements. With quotas, quarter ends, sales meetings, and all the things you deal with in your job, some things get neglected. So my goal is to have all these little things—that make a big difference—in a reference form that you can use and refer to down the road.

And if you see that your production is not where it should be, take a step back and consider if you need to be more attentive to certain aspects of your role.

Are you applying the 42 Rules of Cold Calling Executives?

42 These Are My Rules. What Are Yours?

About the Author

Mari Anne Vanella is the founder and CEO of The Vanella Group, Inc., a Telesales firm serving the high-tech industry based in the Silicon Valley. For over 20 years, Mari Anne has designed and executed outbound calling practices that outperform traditional methods. She has worked with companies such as HP, Borland Software, Cisco, Guidewire Software, Savvion, and many others helping them identify opportunities for their sales organizations.

Write Your Own Rules

You can write your own 42 Rules book, and we can help you do it—from initial concept, to writing and editing, to publishing and marketing. If you have a great idea for a 42 Rules book, then we want to hear from you.

As you know, the books in the 42 Rules series are practical guidebooks that focus on a single topic. The books are written in an easy-to-read format that condenses the fundamental elements of the topic into 42 Rules. They use realistic examples to make their point and are fun to read.

Two Kinds of 42 Rules Books

42 Rules books are published in two formats: the single-author book and the contributed-author book. The single-author book is a traditional book written by one author. The contributed-author book (like *42 Rules for Working Moms*) is a compilation of Rules, each written by a different contributor, which support the main topic. If you want to be the sole author of a book or one of its contributors, we can help you succeed!

42 Rules Program

A lot of people would like to write a book, but only a few actually do. Finding a publisher, and distributing and marketing the book are challenges that prevent even the most ambitious of authors to ever get started.

At 42 Rules, we help you focus on and be successful in the writing of your book. Our program concentrates on the following tasks so you don't have to:

- **Publishing:** You receive expert advice and guidance from the Executive Editor, copy editors, technical editors, and cover and layout designers to help you create your book.

- **Distribution:** We distribute your book through the major book distribution channels, like Baker & Taylor and Ingram, Amazon.com, Barnes and Noble, Borders Books, etc.

- **Marketing:** 42 Rules has a full-service marketing program that includes a customized Web page for you and your book, email registrations and campaigns, blogs, webcasts, media kits and more.

Whether you are writing a single-authored book or a contributed-author book, you will receive editorial support from 42 Rules Executive Editor, Laura Lowell, author of *42 Rules of Marketing*, which was rated Top 5 in Business Humor and Top 25 in Business Marketing on Amazon.com (December 2007), and author and Executive Editor of *42 Rules for Working Moms*.

Accepting Submissions

If you want to be a successful author, we'll provide you the tools to help make it happen. Start today by answering the following questions and visit our website at http://superstarpress.com/ for more information on submitting your 42 Rules book idea.

Super Star Press is now accepting submissions for books in the 42 Rules book series. For more information, email info@superstarpress.com or call 408-257-3000.

Books

Other Happy About Books

Learn the 42 Rules of Marketing!

Compilation of ideas, theories, and practical approaches to marketing challenges that marketers know they should do, but don't always have the time or patience to do.

Paperback $19.95
eBook $11.95

Networking Online— Making LinkedIn Work for you!

This book explains the benefits of using LinkedIn and recommends best practices so that you can get the most out of it.

Paperback: $19.95
eBook: $11.95

Purchase these books at Happy About
http://happyabout.info
or at other online and physical bookstores.

A Message From Super Star Press™

Thank you for your purchase of this 42 Rules Series book. It is available online at: http://happyabout.info/42rules/coldcallingexecutives.php or at other online and physical bookstores. To learn more about contributing to books in the 42 Rules series, check out http://superstarpress.com.

Super Star Press™ is interested in you if you are an author who would like to submit a non-fiction book proposal or a corporation that would like to have a book written for you. Please contact us by email info@superstarpress.com or phone (408-257-3000).

Please contact us for quantity discounts at sales@superstarpress.com

If you want to be informed by email of upcoming books, please email bookupdate@superstarpress.com.

Printed in the United States
213840BV00006B/3/P